FERRIES OF SCOTLAND

ISBN 0 9513093 4 X

This page: The *Isle of Arran* at Ardrossan in August 1990. (Iain McCall)

THE introduction of *SeaCat Scotland* in June 1992 onto the Stranraer – Belfast route is the latest in a long line of developments in the Scottish ferry industry, and it gives me great pleasure to discuss some of them here.

While SeaCat represents the leading edge in ferry technology and has dramatically reduced travelling times between Scotland and Northern Ireland, the nature of many other Scottish services where a ferry often represents the only means of reaching outlying islands means speed is not so crucial. This has led to a rich variety of ferry types around our coast, many of them custom built for the communities and routes they service.

Although SeaCat is the new kid as far as the ferry industry is concerned in this area, I have been involved with shipping for many years both at sea and ashore. It is an industry which is never dull and which has seen tremendous change over the last couple of decades. The impact of the Roll On/Roll Off concept on ferry operation has been vital and has dramatically changed the face of coastal shipping.

During that time the Scottish ferry industry, like most others, has altered greatly, and one of the changes has been the moves towards the private sector. The biggest example of this was the privatisation of Sealink in 1984. There are, of course, still some ferries operating under the banner of Local Authorities and this will continue.

No foreword to a book about Scottish ferries could fail to mention Caledonian MacBrayne. Currently the direct responsibility of the Secretary of State for Scotland, 'Calmac', as it is affectionately termed, is the largest ferry operator in Scotland with a fleet of over 30 vessels providing services around the coast and to many island communities.

Calmac over recent years has transformed its business with a healthy and still ongoing 'newbuild' programme and with a high decree of route inter-changeability built into its larger vessels.

Within the private sector P&O Scottish Ferries, P&O European Ferries and Stena Sealink Line have all made substantial investments in their fleets in recent years. Following a major refit P&O introduced the *St Clair* on the Aberdeen-Lerwick service in March 1992. The *Pride of Rathlin* and the *Pride of Ailsa* were introduced on the Northern Ireland service from Cairnryan, substantially upgrading existing services.

Stena Sealink Line, with the introduction of the *Stena Antrim,* now has an excellent fleet of three Belfast-built 'Saint' class vessels to link up to the considerable improvements in onboard facilities in which they have also invested. All are to be commended for the benefits which have accrued to passengers as a result.

The introduction of *SeaCat Scotland* marks a new and dramatic stage in the development of the Scottish ferry scene. It has been exciting to be involved in the launch of the new service from Stranraer to the heart of Belfast. Following its success, I have no doubt that other SeaCat services will be developed across the Irish Sea in the near future.

This book is a well researched record of the rich variety of ferries trading round the Scottish coast. It is a fascinating read for anyone interested in ships, and I wish it every success.

Hamish Ross
Managing Director, SeaCat Scotland

The SeaCat Experience

Setting the pace across the Irish Sea

From the moment you drive on board SeaCat you know it's special.

Your seat is guaranteed in the superb air-conditioned lounge; and you'll find plenty of room to stretch out and relax.

Wander along to the panoramic bar....... enjoy a snack ....purchase a gift from our on-board selection.

And why not get a unique captain's view from the luxurious observation lounge, or stroll on the rear deck and breathe fresh sea air.

SeaCat

SeaCat – a truly unique experience. From Stranraer to the heart of Belfast, in just 90 minutes, up to 5 times a day.

See your local travel agent or call Hoverspeed reservations on:

Belfast – (0232) 310910
Glasgow – (041) 204 2266

HOVER*SPEED*

This profusely illustrated picture book of past and present 'Ferries of Scotland' was born out of edition number 12 of our quarterly ferry magazine, 'British Ferry Scene'. My partner Miles Cowsill and I decided that this should be a Scottish issue, and we were both surprised and delighted when it became an instant sell-out.

This present publication in no way attempts to cover all present ferries, or indeed all past ones, but it does give a broad sample of the vessels which have served Scotland since the war with the additional inclusion of several even older ships.

My sincere thanks to all those photographers who have kindly sent examples of their work for inclusion within these pages and particularly to the excellent Lawrence Macduff for sharing his extensive collection with us. Thanks are also due to Ian Hall for checking the proofs.

Reading this book will be very much a second-best experience. By far the best way is to sail in the ships themselves and to capture the unique atmosphere of the distant places which many of them serve. We have invited the principal operators to participate in this publication and we warmly thank them for their support.

Haste ye back!

John Hendy

AROUND THE COAST

The Tasmanian-built catamaran *SeaCat Scotland* entered service on the Stranraer – Belfast service in June 1992. Capable of carrying 80 cars and 450 passengers across the North Channel, she offers up to five sailings a day in the high season.

Built in Belfast for the British Railways Board as the fourth of a series of similar vessels, the *St. David* entered service on the Holyhead – Dun Laoghaire route in August 1981. During 1985 she was based at Dover, operating to Ostend, but after the failure of that service was switched to the Stranraer station in 1986. With Stena Line's purchase of Sealink UK Ltd., in 1991 the vessel's name was changed to *Stena Caledonia*. (Miles Cowsill)

The *Stena Galloway* (ex *Galloway Princess*) was the first of the four vessels built in Belfast in 1980/81. She has only left the route on which she entered service in April 1980 on one occasion, when she was called to assist on the Holyhead station during the summer of 1992. (Miles Cowsill)

The *Stena Antrim* (left) was the Dover – Calais vessel *St. Christopher* until reallocated to operate the North Channel link in April 1991. She was the third of the Harland & Wolff quartet to be built. The *European Freighter* was built on the Tyne, as the *Europic Ferry*, for the Atlantic Steam Navigation Co. in 1967. Originally used on the Felixstowe – Europort link, she was later switched to Southampton after the ASN had been absorbed into the European Ferries Group. The 'Europic' was requisitioned for the Falkland Islands Task Force in 1982. Since March 1983 she has been used on the Larne – Cairnryan passage and was renamed *European Freighter* in April 1992. (Miles Cowsill)

The *Pride of Ailsa* was built at Schiedam (Rotterdam) as the *Free Enterprise VI* in 1972 for the European Ferries Group, who placed her in service between Dover and Zeebrugge. During the winter of 1985/86 she was stretched and raised at Bremerhaven giving her capacity for 1035 passengers and 370 cars. After the purchase of the EFG by P&O in 1987, she was renamed *Pride of Sandwich* in the following year and when in March 1992 she was switched to the Larne – Cairnryan link, she received her present name. (Miles Cowsill)

The *Pride of Rathlin* was originally the *Free Enterprise VII* which was built a year later than her sister ship and operating partner. She too was stretched and was later renamed *Pride of Walmer*. She received her present name on her arrival at Larne in June 1992. (Miles Cowsill)

The *Isle of Arran* leaving Ardrossan for Brodick, Arran, in June 1986. She was built at Port Glasgow in 1984 and will be replaced by a larger vessel during 1993, at which time she is due to transfer to the Islay station allowing the *Claymore* to work the summer only Mallaig – Armadale (Skye) route. (David Parsons)

Quick Quick

Slow

When you cruise across to Northern Ireland with P&O European Ferries, you'll find Cairnryan
to Larne is the shortest crossing . . . but we don't stop short on service.

Our two improved ships are bigger and better in every way, with stylish decor and superb
facilities, and for just a little extra you can enjoy the exclusive luxury of our Club Class.

By the time you've reached Northern Ireland we guarantee you'll be in the perfect mood to enjoy
the gentle lakes, quiet roads, golden sands and miles of unspoilt scenery that lie ahead.

When it comes to friendly chat and lively entertainment you'll find
Northern Ireland doesn't stop short either.

For reservations or further information call Cairnryan (05812) 276.

Only P&O European Ferries lets you cruise the shortest crossing in style.

P&O
European Ferries

The skipper of the *Loch Ranza* at her Voith-Schneider controls. (Brian Maxted)

The new *Loch Tarbert* took up the secondary Arran service from Lochranza (Arran) to Claonaig in July 1992. (Lawrence Macduff)

The *Loch Striven* was the lead ship of four sisters built on the Humber in 1986. She is presently engaged on the Largs – Cumbrae Slip service with sistership *Loch Linnhe*.

Maintaining the secondary Bute service across the famous Kyles of Bute is the *Loch Riddon*, seen here leaving Colintraive for Rhubodach in August 1989. (John Hendy)

The *Jupiter* entered service on the Gourock – Dunoon car ferry in March 1974. She is seen here leaving the Cowal resort in August 1982. (Colin Smith)

The splendour of the upper Firth of Clyde can be appreciated in this view of the *Juno* crossing to Gourock in November 1985. (Lawrence Macduff)

The third of the Clyde 'streakers' was the *Saturn* which was originally used on the Wemyss Bay – Rothesay (Bute) service but today works in tandem with her two half-sisters. (John Hendy)

Western Ferries (Clyde) operate the shorter Cowal crossing between McInroy's Point and Hunter's Quay. The *Sound of Scarba* was built in Sweden as the *Olandssund III* in 1960 but was sold to Western Ferries in 1973 following the opening of a new bridge. She is now the relief vessel. (Lawrence Macduff)

Built as the *Olandssund IV*, the *Sound of Shuna* came to Scotland during the same period as her smaller fleet companion. She opened the new Cowal link in June 1973. (Lawrence Macduff)

The *Sound of Seil* dates from 1959, when she was built as the *Freshwater* for the British Railways (Southern Region) service between Lymington and Yarmouth (Isle of Wight). Replaced by larger tonnage in 1983, she eventually came north in 1986 and entered service in June. (Richard Kilbey)

The most recent addition to the Western Ferries fleet is the *Sound of Sleat*. She was originally the *De Hoorn* and was built in 1961 to operate across the New Waterway in Holland. She has operated on the upper Firth of Clyde since 1988. (Richard Kilbey)

The Clyde Marine Motoring Company acquired their *Kenilworth* from the Hythe – Southampton ferry, where she operated as the *Hotspur II*, in 1978. Dating from 1936 the vessel has capacity for 150 persons and operates on the Gourock – Kilcreggan service which is extended to Helensburgh during the summer months. (C.M.M.Co.)

The Second Snark was built in 1938 by the Dumbarton shipyard of Wm. Denny & Bros. for whom she was their tender. She replaced an older vessel, The *Snark* of 1882, but retained her odd Lewis Carroll name after Denny's went into liquidation in 1963 and she was purchased by her present owners in 1969. She is seen arriving at Dunoon from Largs during August 1989. (John Hendy)

A third Clyde Marine Motoring Co's vessel is the *Rover* which has a certificate for 120 passengers and dates from 1964 when she was built at Renfrew. She is engaged on tender work with relief sailings on the Gourock – Kilcreggan service. (C.M.M.Co)

The preserved paddle steamer *Waverley* is the most widely travelled of all such vessels, having circumnavigated Britain bringing the lost delights of big ship coastal cruising to thousands. Built on the Clyde in 1947, the *Waverley* was sold to the Paddle Steamer Preservation Society for £1 in 1974. The rest is history. (John Hendy)

Caledonian MacBrayne's ubiquitous small Island class of car ferry are common sights on Scotland's west coast, serving and providing access to many small communities with their capacity for 50 passengers and 6 cars. The *Rhum* today serves as a relief vessel. (Walter Bowie)

Maintaining the 5-minute link across the Sound of Islay between Feolin (Jura) and Port Askaig (Islay) is Western Ferries (Arygll), *Sound of Gigha*. Built as the *Isle of Gigha* in 1966, she was purchased and renamed three years later, (David Parsons)

The *Iona* is now Caledonian MacBrayne's oldest large car ferry having been built at Troon in 1970. Originally built for the Islay link she was not to serve this route until 1979, having served on a variety of services between times. Today she is the summer Mallaig – Armadale (Skye) ferry, although with new tonnage due her future is now in doubt. (Brian Maxted)

Strathclyde Regional Council operates the *Balnahua* between Seil and Luing. Capable of carrying 5 cars and 40 passengers, the vessel was built at Campbeltown in 1973. (Brian Maxted)

On 7th March 1989 the new Oban – Outer Isles car ferry, *Lord of the Isles,* was launched at Port Glasgow. She entered service on the Oban – Lochboisdale (South Uist) – Castlebay (Barra) link in May 1989 and in the following month included Oban – Coll and Tiree into her rosters. (Lawrence Macduff)

Seen on passage between Castlebay (Barra) and Oban during July 1991, the bridge of the *Lord of the Isles* certainly makes an impressive sight. (Dick Clague)

Arriving at Fionnphort (Mull) from the Sacred Isle of Iona (background) is the Island class ferry, *Morvern*. (Lawrence Macduff)

The *Loch Buie* was especially built for the Iona service and entered service during June 1992. (Lawrence Macduff)

Island class ferries *Rhum* and *Eigg* together at Oban's Railway Pier in June 1992. (Richard Kilbey)

The *Isle of Mull* is the primary link between Oban and Craignure (Mull). She was built at Port Glasgow in 1988, but serious deadweight problems saw an extra 20 ft. added to her hull the following winter. She carries 1000 passengers and 80 cars. (Walter Bowie)

Since 1986, the *Isle of Cumbrae* has served the secondary route to Mull via Lochaline (Morvern) and Fishnish although she was built for the island whose name she carries in 1977. She is seen here at Cumbrae Slip. (Walter Bowie)

Built as one of a trio of ships for MacBrayne's Western Isles car ferry services, the *Columba* was placed on the Oban – Craignure (Mull) – Lochaline route in July 1964. Finally sold out of service in 1988, she was purchased by Hebridean Island Cruises and converted to her present cruising role as the *Hebridean Princess*. She is seen here at Oban in September 1991. (Nick Robins)

Seen arriving at Castlebay on the island of Barra in June 1984, the car ferry *Claymore* passes the turntable ferry *Glenmallie*. Formerly of Glenelg, the latter vessel served the island of Vatersay (south of Barra) before finally being abandoned there. (David Hewitt)

The Highland Regional Council operate the Corran – Ardgour link across Loch Linnhe with the *Maid of Glencoul* and the *Rosehaugh* (left). The former was replaced from the Kylesku – Kylestrome ferry (Sutherland) in 1984 while the latter came from the South Kessock – North Kessock link to the Black Isle in 1982. Both were made redundant by bridges. (Lawrence Macduff)

Now one of the few passenger-only ferries in operation around our shores, the *Lochmor* was built at Troon in 1979 to operate the Mallaig – Armadale (Skye) – Small Isles link. (Lawrence Macduff)

Since 1989, the *Pioneer* has been Caledonian MacBrayne's spare unit. She is seen here on 21st June 1979 when approaching Armadale (Skye) and immediately after she had retracted her stabilisers. Even in summer the weather can be unkind! (Lawrence Macduff)

The last of a long line. The privately owned turntable ferry *Glenachulish* operates the summer-only link across the Sound of Sleat between Glenelg and Kylerhea (Skye). She was built in 1969 for the Ballachulish ferry but was replaced by a bridge in 1975. After serving as a relief ferry for the Highland Regional Council, she passed to the present link in 1984. (James Newton)

The *Loch Dunvegan* (illustrated) and sistership *Loch Fyne* entered service on the Kyle of Lochalsh – Kyleakin (Skye) service during 1991. They too, are due to be replaced by a bridge. (Walter Bowie)

The last of the small Island class car ferries was the *Raasay* which since 1976 has operated between Sconser (Skye) and the island whose name she carries. (Bernard McCall)

At the north end of Skye lies Uig, the ferry terminal for Tarbert (Harris) and Lochmaddy (North Uist). Built in Selby in 1985, the *Hebridean Isles* took up station in May 1986 after roll-on facilities had been constructed at her ports of call. She is seen here off Uig in April 1989. (Lawrence Macduff)

Replaced by the *Isle of Cumbrae* on the Lochaline – Fishnish link in 1986, the Island class ferry *Canna* was used as a relief ship until being transferred to the Kyles Scalpay (Harris) – Scalpay service four years later. She is seen approaching Kyles Scalpay in July of that year. (Bernard McCall)

The Western Isles Council operate two pale-blue hulled, ferries. The *Eilean Na H-Oige* is used on the Ludaig (South Uist) to Eriskay service. Built at Stornoway in 1980, she is seen loading at Ludaig in June 1984. (David Hewitt)

The *Eilean Bhearnaraigh* (meaning Island of Berneray) is seen at Newtonferry (North Uist) arriving from Berneray. She was constructed in Glasgow in 1983. (Brian Maxted)

The northern outpost of the Caledonian MacBrayne empire is the crossing of the Minch between Ullapool and Stornoway (Lewis). Since 1974, the service has been operated by the Norwegian-built ferry *Suilven* which is seen here while on relief at Oban during October 1989. (Lawrence Macduff)

Built as the Swedish ferry *Svea Scarlett* in 1971, the fourth *St. Ola* entered service on P&O Scottish Ferries Pentland Firth link between Scrabster and Stromness (Orkney) in March 1992. Although older than the *St. Ola* (IV) that she replaced, her extra size gives greater comfort and capacity on the route. She is seen here off Holborn Head in May 1992. (Lawrence Macduff)

Overleaf: The car ferry *Caledonia* (ex *Stena Baltica*) arrived on station in 1970, first being used on the Ardrossan – Brodick link. She moved to Oban for summer runs to Craignure (Mull) six years later and she is seen here leaving Oban Bay and heading out into the Firth of Lorn. She was sold out of service in 1988. (Lawrence Macduff)

In service between Invergordon and Kirkwall (Orkney), the maroon-hulled roll-on vessel *Contender* commenced service in March 1992 in opposition to the established Aberdeen link of P&O Scottish Ferries. Formerly the *Indiana*, the vessel operated a service between Argentina and the Falkland Islands prior to taking up her present role. (Willie MacKay)

A summer-only 45-minute link between John O'Groats and the Orkney village of Burwick (South Ronaldsay) is provided by the passenger vessel *Pentland Venture*. Built in 1987, this view predates the vessel's stretching by 21 ft. during 1991. (Lawrence Macduff)

The *Hoy Head* (seen off Lyness in July 1991) was built as the *Geira* for the Shetland Islands Council in 1973. Replaced by larger tonnage, she passed to the Orkney Islands Shipping Company in 1986, being placed on the South Isles service between Houton (Mainland) and Lyness (Hoy), Flotta and Longhope (South Walls). Replaced by the *Thorsvoe* in 1991, she is now the spare vessel. (Lawrence Macduff)

The *Thorsvoe* is seen at Houton in August 1992 having been built at Campbeltown in the previous year. Her capacity is for 96 passengers and 16 cars against the 93 passengers and 10 cars of the ship she replaced. (Lawrence Macduff)

Built in Bristol in 1987, the *Eynhallow* works the ferry service between Tingwall (Mainland) and the islands of Rousay, Egilsay and Wyre. Such was her success that in 1991 she was lengthened to increase carrying capacity. (Ian Hall)

The OISCo's *Shapinsay* was built in Hull during 1989 for the Kirkwall to Shapinsay service. She is seen here at the Balfour slip on her home island during August 1990. (Lawrence Macduff)

The sisters *Earl Sigurd* and *Earl Thorfinn* were built on the Mersey and entered service during 1990 to commence roll-on operations to the North Isles between Kirkwall and Eday, Papa Westray, Sanday, Stronsay, Westray and North Ronaldsay. Here the 'Sigurd' is seen near Kirkwall in August 1992. (Lawrence Macduff)

The *Varagen* came to the OISCo second-hand being built for the ill-fated company Orkney Ferries who had hoped to establish a new service between Gill's Bay (Caithness) and Burwick (South Ronaldsay). The vessel was acquired in 1991 and now runs in tandem with the *Earl Thorfinn* and *Earl Sigurd*. (Nick Robins)

Shetland Islands Council

MARINE OPERATIONS DEPARTMENT FERRY DIVISION
PORT ADMINISTRATION BUILDING
SELLA NESS, GRAVEN, MOSSBANK, SHETLAND ZE2 9QR
TEL: SULLOM VOE (0806) 242551 EXT. 256.
FAX: (0806) 242237. TELEX: 75142.

The *Fivla* was built for the Shetland Islands Council at Troon in 1985 for the services linking Gutcher (Yell) to Belmont (Unst) and Gutcher to Oddsta (Fetla). She can accommodate 95 passengers and 15 cars. (Lawrence Macduff)

The *Hendra* dates from 1982 and maintains the link between Laxo (Mainland) and Symbister (Whalsay). She is seen here at Symbister in October 1991. (Lawrence Macduff)

One of the original series of Shetland Islands car ferries still in service is the *Thora*, although today she is retained as the spare vessel. She is seen here in Yell Sound in October 1991. (Lawrence Macduff)

The tiny *Filla* is the ferry to Out Skerries, two islands 25 miles east of Mainland Shetland. Capable of carrying just 12 passengers and 6 cars, this vessel provides a vital link for the 70 people remaining on the islands. (Lawrence Macduff)

The *Grima* is another of the original Shetland ferries being used on the Lerwick – Maryfield (Bressay) link. (Lawrence Macduff)

Between Orkney and Shetland lies lonely Fair Isle which is served by the *Good Shepherd IV* from her base at Grutness (Mainland). As can be seen, loading vehicles is a specialist occupation. She was built at St. Monan's, Fife in 1986. (John Phillips)

The previous Fair Isle vessel was built as a trawler in 1969 until purchased by the islanders and named *Good Shepherd III*. After her replacement by the present ship, at which time the Shetland Islands Council took over the running of the service, she was purchased by them and renamed *Koada*. Today she operates between West Burrafirth (Mainland) and Papa Stour and Foula. Her successor, the *Westering Homewards*, has been rejected by the SIC. (John Phillips)

Used on the route between Toft (Mainland) and Ulsta (Yell) are the ferries, *Geira* (left) and *Bigga*, dating from 1988 and 1991. They are seen here at Ulsta in 1991. (David Parsons)

68 The oldest of the SIC ferries is the former Norwegian fjord vessel *Kjella* which dates from 1957. Acquired by the SIC in 1980, she is now a reserve vessel. She is seen here approaching Toft in May 1991. (Lawrence Macduff)

The freight ferry *St. Rognvald* was built in Germany in 1970. After a number of name changes, she was chartered to P&O Scottish Ferries during 1989, then being called *Marino Torre*. The following year she was purchased and renamed *St. Rognvald* and is today engaged on services between Aberdeen Stromness, Kirkwall and Lerwick. (John Phillips)

The *St. Sunniva* was built in Denmark in 1971 as the *Djursland* before being renamed *Lasse II* three years later. During 1979 she was sold to P&O Ferries for service between Dover and Boulogne where she served as the *nf Panther*. After the ships and service were sold to the European Ferries Group in 1985, she was replaced in the following year before being sold back to P&O in 1987. On conversion from a day to an overnight ferry, she was renamed *St. Sunniva* and serves Aberdeen, Stromness and Lerwick. She is seen leaving Aberdeen in May 1991. (Lawrence Macduff)

Superior accommodation with spectacular sea views.

When you sail to Orkney and Shetland with P&O Scottish Ferries you'll be spoilt with the high standards of comfort and service on the way to these unspoilt islands as well as by spectacular views from the sea of the coastline, wild yet gentle and inviting in its solitude.

Our latest vessels St Clair and St Ola, like their sister ship St Sunniva are as much a part of the local scene as the seabirds and the seals and ensure the perfect start to your island adventure.

You can choose from hotel inclusive holidays, mini-cruises, motorist holidays or day excursions. Our regular sailing prices start from £13.00.

Whichever you decide, you'll find us more than accommodating.

For further information see your local travel agent or contact P&O Scottish Ferries, Jamieson's Quay, Aberdeen, AB9 8DL. Tel: (0224) 572615.

P&O Scottish Ferries

Leaving Aberdeen for Stavanger in May 1992, the latest *St. Clair* boasts an interesting history. Built as the *Travemunde* in 1971 for a Denmark – Germany link, she was later sold to Yugoslavia (where she served as the *Njegos*) before being renamed *Tregastel* when taken on charter by Brittany Ferries in 1985. Two years later she was purchased and remained in the fleet until 1991 when sold to P&O Scottish Ferries to replace the previous *St. Clair*. She entered service on the Aberdeen – Lerwick link in March 1992. (Lawrence Macduff)

Built in 1987, the *Cromarty Rose* is owned by Seaboard Marine (Nigg) and carries 2 cars across the Cromarty Firth between Cromarty, in the Black Isle, and Nigg in Easter Ross. (Jeremy Hartill)

The catamaran *Spirit of Fife* is operated by Forth Ferry Services and was formerly the Channel Islands vessel *Herm Trident IV*. She arrived at Granton in March 1991 and carries up to 250 passengers across the Firth of Forth to Burntisland. She is seen here on the Fife bank in March 1991. (Ian Hall)

The *Ionic Ferry* was built in France in 1967 as the *Dragon* for the new P&O Normandy Ferries service between Southampton and Le Havre. Due to lack of traffic in the early years, she frequently cruised to Portugal and as far afield as north Africa. The Le Havre service was transferred to Portsmouth before the *Dragon* – and sister *Leopard* – were purchased by the European Ferries Group in 1985. She was transferred to the Larne – Cairnryan link in June 1986 and renamed *Ionic Ferry*, but stood down with the arrival of the *Pride of Rathlin* in June 1992. She has since sailed to Greece as the *Viscountess M*, once again taking up service with her sister, *Countess M*. (Miles Cowsill)

The *Darnia* was originally the *Stena Topper*, built on the Danube in Austria, and entered service at Stranraer in August 1978. During spring 1982 she was sent to Immingham where her passenger accommodation was increased to 400, a move which was to cause problems with her stability following new guidelines issued after the Zeebrugge ferry disaster five years later. She was therefore sold to Swedish owners, completing her final sailing in February 1991, and operates today as the *Nord Neptunus*. (Miles Cowsill)

The first of many! The chartered *Stena Nordica* on service for British Rail across the North Channel between Stranraer and Larne in 1966 – 71. (Andrew Knox)

Ardrossan was the summer base for the Isle of Man Steam Packet Company's service. Here is the turbine passenger steamer *Mona's Isle* (of 1951) leaving for Douglas in July 1979. (Joe McKendrick)

Built by Fairfield at Govan in 1936, the *Marchioness of Graham* operated on the Ardrossan – Brodick (Arran) service until replaced by the *Glen Sannox* in 1957. Her extensive deck space was ideal for the carriage of cars. She was sold to Greece and renamed *Hellas*. (J. Graeme Bruce)

The *Glen Sannox* was a much-travelled and much-loved vehicle ferry. Built for the Arran run in 1957, she was replaced by the *Caledonia* in 1970 after which she moved up firth to cover the two other car ferry links before appearing on the Oban – Craignure link in 1974. She then became a Clyde cruise ship from 1978 before becoming the winter Oban – Mull relief vessel in 1982. Finally sold in 1989, she sailed to Greece as the *Knooz*. She is seen here off Brodick in September 1988. (Lawrence Macduff)

The *Kilbrannan* was the first and smallest of the eight small Island class car ferries. Entering service for the Caledonian Steam Packet Company in 1972, she commenced working on the new link connecting Lochranza (Arran) and Claonaig. Since that time she served on a number of routes, latterly at Kyles Scalpay (Harris) before becoming the relief vessel. During 1992, she was sold to the Republic of Ireland for a service linking Burtonpoint (Co. Donegal) and Leabgarrow (Arranmore Islands). (C. McClenahan)

The *King Edward* was the first passenger ship in the world to be propelled by steam turbines, and must therefore rank as one of the most famous of all Scottish steamers. Built at Denny's in 1901, she lasted a magnificent fifty years until being broken up at Troon in 1952. She is seen off Kirn during the summer of 1949. (A.M. Young)

The London, Midland and Scottish Railway introduced the paddle steamer *Jupiter* in 1937. She was originally used for the railway connected services between Greenock and the Kyles of Bute via (inter alia) Gourock, Dunoon, Wemyss Bay and Rothesay. The large space between her funnels allowed vehicles to be stowed and later in her career she worked between Wemyss Bay and Rothesay (Bute) until replaced by the car ferry *Bute*. Her final season was 1957, and she was broken up in Dublin four years later. (A.M. Young)

The *Caledonia* of 1934 survived in service until 1969. She was built at Denny's Dumbarton yard for the M.S. railway connected services from Greenock, Gourock and Wemyss Bay. Replaced by the ABC car ferries in 1954, she became the Ayr excursion steamer, also ferrying when required on the Ardrossan – Arran link. Purchased by Charrington's Brewery for floating pub duties on the Thames, she was damaged by fire in 1980, following which she was broken up near Sittingbourne, Kent. Her engines have happily been preserved. (David Parsons)

The *Keppel* was originally the British Railways (Eastern Region) passenger ferry *Rose*. Built at Southampton with her sisters *Catherine* and *Edith*, she took up the Tilbury – Gravesend link in 1961. With the Dartford Tunnel under the Thames seriously affecting loadings, she was 'sold' to the Caledonian Steam Packet Co. in 1967, becoming the Largs – Millport (Cumbrae) ferry. After the termination of the service in 1986 she continued as a summer cruise vessel until her withdrawal at the close of her 1992 season. (David Parsons)

The *Maid of Cumbrae* was one of four 'Maids' (the others being Ashton, Argyll and Skelmorlie) which were built for the CSP in 1953 for the high frequency services on the Upper Firth. By the late sixties, many of the small piers to which she had worked were closed and the ship was eventually laid up until it was decided to convert her to a car ferry. She re-entered service in May 1972. For her new role on the Gourock – Dunoon link she was capable of carrying 15 cars, but she was retired and became the spare vessel following the entry into service of the *Juno* in December 1974. She was sold four years later to Italian buyers. (Lawrence Macduff)

The *Arran* (and her sisters *Bute* and *Cowal*) were the first car ferries built for use in western Scotland. She was launched in September 1953 and entered service on the Gourock – Dunoon crossing in the following January. In 1970 she was switched to the West Loch Tarbert – Islay route and two years later underwent a major conversion which replaced her hoist method of loading to roll-on – roll-off. Replaced on the Islay route by the *Pioneer* in 1974, she became a relief ship until sold for static use in Dublin. Since removed to Manchester, the vessel has certainly seen better days. (David Parsons)

This picture of the *Cowal* off Gourock in April 1973 illustrates how sistership *Arran* looked before her conversion. She was the second of the ABC car ferries to enter service and the only one to serve all her days on the Clyde. She was sold to Greek owners in 1979. (Lawrence Macduff)

The Bute Ferry Co's car ferry *Eilean Mhor* was originally a wartime landing craft but earned the distinction of becoming the first car ferry on the Kyles of Bute service between Rhubodach and Colintraive. She commenced service in July 1950, although the Caledonian S.P. Co. took over the operation twenty years later. (J. Graeme Bruce)

The C.S.P. took over the operation of the secondary Bute crossing in 1970 and transferred and converted the former Kyle of Lochalsh – Skye ferries *Portree* (of 1965) and *Broadford* (of 1966) to the route. They were sold for further service when the new *Loch Riddon* entered service in 1986. (Brian Maxted)

February 1987 saw the *Columba* and *Caledonia* laid-up for the winter in the James Watt Dock at Greenock. (Lawrence Macduff)

A reminder of the many fine Clyde-built vessels which graced our shores for so long. Here is the launch of the Stranraer – Larne car ferry *Caledonian Princess* for Caledonian Steam Packet (Irish Services) Ltd. at Denny's Dumbarton yard on 5th April 1961. Later becoming British Rail's most travelled vessel, she ended service at Dover in September 1981 before seeing static use at Newcastle and more recently at Glasgow. (Wm. Ralston & Co.)

The Isle of Man Steam Packet Co's last passenger turbine steamer *Manxman* (of 1955) at Yorkhill Quay, Glasgow for a refit in Spring 1980. Withdrawn in 1982, she is today in static use in Liverpool. (Joe McKendrick)

One of Scotland's strangest ferries! The *Vehicular Ferryboat No. 3* entered service in 1908 from the Ferguson Bros. yard at Port Glasgow. The Finnieston ferry was provided with an elevating platform which was raised or lowered to suit the tidal conditions thereby eliminating the need for a linkspan. The service was withdrawn in 1966. (J. Graeme Bruce)

During the paddle steamer *Waverley's* fortieth year, she was withdrawn with mechanical problems and was replaced by the Sealink Isle of Wight services motor vessel *Southsea*. Built at Denny's in 1948, she had adopted a cruising role in the Solent during 1987. A hastily arranged charter saw the *Southsea* arrive at Anderston Quay on 5th September 1987. This view, taken from the *Waverley*, shows the *Southsea* swinging by the Kingston Bridge. (Joe McKendrick)

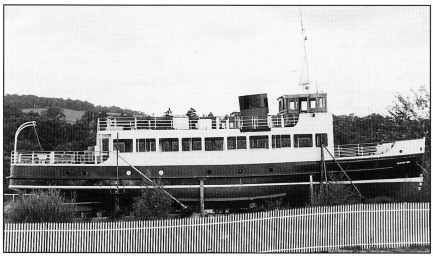

Formerly of Loch Awe, the 1936-built *Countess of Breadalbane* was brought to the Clyde in 1952, operating on a variety of routes including Rothesay and Tighnabruaich, Wemyss Bay – Innellan and Largs – Millport. After her sale in 1971 she became the *Countess of Kempock* before further purchase by the Alloa Brewery Co. and removal to Loch Lomond where she adopted the name of *Countess Fiona*. This view sees her laid up at Balloch in August 1992, having not operated since 1989. (Dave Hocquard)

The launch *Loch Shiel* was built in 1953 for David MacBrayne Ltd. for service in the loch whose name she bore (between Moidart and Sunart). She was based at the railway linked settlement of Glenfinnan for nine years before she was switched to operate the cargo runs to Iona. Additionally, she ferried up to 62 passengers ashore from the excursion steamers at anchor out in the Sound of Iona where this picture was taken. (A.M. Young)

The turbine steamer *King George V* enjoyed a 49-year career, most of which was spent based on the West Highland port of Oban. Dating from 1926, the steamer was built for Turbine Steamers Ltd, being sold to MacBrayne's nine years later. Here she is at anchor in the Sound of Iona in June 1973 as passengers return from the island in readiness for a traditional MacBrayne High Tea. (John Hendy)

Hall, Russell & Co. of Aberdeen built the first three car ferries for service in the Western Isles. The *Hebrides, Clansman* and *Columba* all entered service during 1964, the *Clansman* between Mallaig and Armadale (Skye). During winter spells she relieved on the Stornoway (Lewis) link and deputised for her sisters on the Uig (Skye) – Lochmaddy (North Uist) – Tarbert (Harris), and Oban – Craignure (Mull) – Lochaline services. In the winter of 1972-73 she was converted to drive-through operations and lengthened by 36 ft for service on the Ullapool – Stornoway link and in 1976 moved to the Ardrossan – Brodick (Arran) crossing. Sold in 1984 to Torbay Seaways, she then passed to Malta before sailing east as the *Al Hussein*. (Lawrence Macduff)

The *Columba* was built for the Oban – Craignure (Mull) – Lochaline link which she commenced in July 1964. Following her sister's conversion to drive-through in 1973, the *Columba* moved northwards to take her place at Mallaig, but the withdrawal of the *King George V* at Oban two years later saw her return to Oban for the rest of her career. During off-season periods she was used elsewhere and in 1979 and in 1980 voyaged to the remote outlier of St. Kilda – 40 miles west of the Outer Hebrides. Sold in 1988, she was purchased by Hebridean Island Cruises (see page 25). She is seen here leaving Oban in August 1986. (Lawrence Macduff)

The cargo vessel *Loch Ard* was built for MacBrayne at Port Glasgow in 1955, entering service on the fortnightly Glasgow – Outer Hebrides service. Latterly associated with the Islay link, this view shows her at Oban's North Pier. (John M. Guy)

Seen here tendering to the *King George V* off Tobermory in June 1973 (because the Inner Isles mail vessel *Claymore* is at the pier), the *Lochnell* was built as a hospital launch in 1941. Sold to MacBrayne's in 1947, she became the Lismore Island ferry until 1964 when for four years she was used in a variety of work. In 1968 she was moved to Tobermory to operate across the Sound of Mull to Mingary on Ardnamurchan. She was sold in 1981, but is still in the Western Highlands working on Loch Leven. (John Hendy)

The *Kyleakin* (and sister vessel *Lochalsh*) were built in Newport (Gwent) for the five-minute crossing to Skye. Capable of carrying 28 cars, the *Kyleakin* was first on station in August 1970 and both remained there until replaced by the larger *Loch Dunvegan* and *Loch Fyne* in 1991. They were sold to Marine Transport Services of Ireland for a new service across the Western Channel, off Cork Harbour. The *Kyleakin* has been renamed *Carrigaloe*, the *Lochalsh* – *Glenbrook*. (Bernard McCall)

The turntable ferry *Queen of Kylesku* was built for the Sutherland County Council in 1967 for service between Unapool and Kylestrome. Ownership was later transferred to the Highland Regional Council but she was laid aside when the new bridge closed yet another ferry service in July 1984. She is seen here in April 1984. (Highland Regional Council)

The third *St. Ola* was built in 1975 for the two-hour crossing of the Pentland Firth between Scrabster (Thurso) and Stromness (Orkney). She is seen here in March 1992 at the end of her career with P&O having been renamed *St. Ola II* in readiness for her successor. (Jim Calder)

INDEX

Isle of Mull	88	CalMac	24	Cromarty Rose	87	Seaboard Marine	45
Isle of Cumbrae	77	CalMac	24	Spirit of Fife	84	Forth Ferries	46
Hebridean Princess	64	Heb. Island Crs	25	*Ionic Ferry*	*67*	*P&O Euro Ferries*	*46*
Claymore	78	CalMac	38	*Darnia*	*77*	*Sealink U.K.*	*47*
Maid of Glencoul	75	Highland R.C.	26	*Stena Nordica**	*65*	*Stena Line*	*47*
Rosehaugh	67	Highland R.C.	26	*Mona's Isle*	*51*	*I.O.M.S.P. Co.*	*48*
Lochmor	79	CalMac	26	*Marchioness of Graham*	*36*	*Caledonian S.P.*	*48*
Pioneer	74	CalMac	27	*Glen Sannox*	*57*	*CalMac*	*49*
Glenachulish	69	Glenelg-Kylerhea	27	*Kilbrannan*	*72*	*CalMac*	*49*
Loch Dunvegan	91	CalMac	28	*King Edward*	*01*	*Caledonian S.P.*	*50*
Raasay	76	CalMac	28	*Jupiter*	*37*	*Caledonian S.P.*	*50*
Hebridean Isles	85	CalMac	29	*Caledonia*	*34*	*Caledonian S.P.*	*51*
Canna	73	CalMac	29	*Caledonia*	*66*	*CalMac 32,54*	
Eilean Na H-Oige	80	W. Isles Council	30	*Keppel*	*60*	*CalMac*	*51*
Eilean Bhearnaraigh	83	W. Isles Council	30	*Maid of Cumbrae*	*53*	*CalMac*	*52*
Suilven	74	CalMac	31	*Arran*	*53*	*CalMac*	*52*
St. Ola	71	P&O Scot Ferries	31	*Cowal*	*54*	*CalMac*	*53*
Contender	73	Orcargo	34	*Eilean Mhor*	*4x*	*Bute Ferry Co.*	*53*
Pentland Venture	87	Thomas & Bews	34	*Broadford*	*66*	*CalMac*	*54*
Hoy Head	73	Orkney Is.S.Co.	35	*Columba*	*64*	*CalMac 54,59*	
Thorsvoe	91	Orkney Is.S.Co.	35	*Caledonian Princess*	*61*	*Sealink U.K.*	*55*
Eynhallow	87	Orkney Is.S.Co.	36	*Manxman*	*55*	*I.O.M.S.P. Co.*	*56*
Shapinsay	89	Orkney Is.S.Co.	36	*Vehicular Ferryboat No.3*	*08*	*Clyde Port Auth.*	*56*
Earl Sigurd	90	Orkney Is.S.Co.	37	*Southsea**	*48*	*Sealink U.K.*	*57*
Varagen	89	Orkney Is.S.Co.	37	*Countess Fiona*	*36*	*Alloa Brewery Co.*	*57*
Fivla	85	Shetland Is.C.	38	*Loch Shiel*	*53*	*David MacBrayne*	*58*
Hendra	82	Shetland Is.C.	39	*King George V*	*26*	*CalMac*	*58*
Thora	75	Shetland Is.C.	39	*Clansman*	*64*	*CalMac*	*59*
Filla	83	Shetland Is.C.	40	*Loch Ard*	*55*	*David MacBrayne*	*60*
Grima	74	Shetland Is.C.	40	*Lochnell*	*41*	*David MacBrayne*	*60*
Good Shepherd IV	86	Shetland Is.C.	41	*Kyleakin*	*70*	*CalMac*	*61*
Koada	69	Shetland Is.C.	41	*Queen of Kylesku*	*67*	*Highland R.C.*	*62*
Bigga	91	Shetland Is.C.	42	*St. Ola II*	*74*	*P&O Scot Ferries*	*62*
Geira	88	Shetland Is.C.	42				
Kjella	57	Shetland Is.C.	42				
St. Rognvald	70	P&O Scot Ferries	43				
St. Sunniva	71	P&O Scot Ferries	43				
St. Clair	71	P&O Scot Ferries	45				

+ denotes final operator or owner whilst on charter in Scotland.

* denotes on charter

Italicised names denote vessels in 'All our Yesterdays'.

BRITISH FERRY SCENE

Our quarterly magazine is packed with facts, photographs and details of everything that's going on in the world of British ferries. The 48 pages are eagerly awaited by both enthusiasts and those who work in the industry. If you're interested in ferries then this magazine is a MUST!

ISSN 0958-1863

Annual subscription £9.70 (UK), £11.20 (Europe & Eire), Overseas: £19.20 (Airmail), £11.20 (Surface mail)

 Available from Ferry Publications